Irredenta

Nightboat Books
New York

Irredenta

Oscar Oswald

ISBN: 978-1-64362-113-5

Cover illustration by Bijou Karman
Design and typesetting by Rissa Hochberger
Typeset in Cardinal Photo and Janson

Cataloging-in-publication data is available
from the Library of Congress

Nightboat Books
New York

www.nightboat.org

CONTENTS

living state fall down

my love far off and quiet as a citizen

no quiet place   no burden to surrender

SHEPHERD'S SONG

Who goes out anyone
unmoors across the border or in solid fog

how is my love
I go anywhere besides

what drones in question,
what shade do I enjoy

who faces west, fleets into citizen
is my preliminary, is none the hearing of

shy of my hearing of America
the idle car and airforce overhead

I name one leaf example
woodcut with the shepherd falls

whitewater page
goodbye recorded thought

Irredenta

THE YOUNG HERDSMAN

Rosemary my atlas, each thread inaudible

what choice to flip the page available

and see behind the mountain how it's done —

first open space make inroads makeshift towns

that coins the land, arrests construction off the highway

whereby each coast is affluent beyond its means

whose forest roads I measure clear I cut back every mile

takes the saddle summer grass and Saddle Mountain

absent trees the distance of one year since harvest

nothing that my source cannot make due without

within my love's domain, my place the furthest possible

my paper gasoline dry depths of pavement

present tense or bristlecone, and in more time

each summer once the heat is broken by the pine

spare parts become common, and to include them

commonplace

To phone my memo driftwood, know mailbox lavender

my source is lost and found by my free hands let go

outside the vehicle, oncoming more empty, outgoes the same

will be pedestrian, picking oranges in the monastery

incoming Thoreau that playa tilts to skyward

nothing locks in place, yet does my trumpet play

what though I open question I exits companion

mourning country, I surrender helpless skipping stones

into thin air like cottonballs beneath the cottonwoods

I play the notes available, resistance rivers arrowheads

what empty patch is not mosaic in the searchlight

my fluke is further west, its aspens that I breathe them here

that I resists the editor their introduction

rendezvous where stream falls from a pipe

"So there is one thought *for the field, another for the house. I would have my thoughts, like wild apples, to be food for walkers, and will not warrant them to be palatable, if tasted in the house"*

Direct me leave abroad what is not here

rainwater and in range the more available

the further my circumference is wrong-footed.

Puddles untether leaves, who then I am

that ends the scene adrift from my apartment.

I speak no civil hex.

I carry beargrass in my pocket, aspen in my earshot

to what furthest I can stray, no statesman

I tune up my pipe with grease and gasoline.

Being without center, who goes elsewhere is the same

freshwater thunderstorm outstanding rain

as I touch timber touch my hand

will this interior be spoken.

I hear flute.

People are Americans.

I song with those who are not made their destinies.

That is true north where I receive it.

I will conclude after the outline I

my fruitless labor —

goodbye crossfire language draws to bow

EXETER

Walk to wood fairweather citizen

stand upstream headwater absentee —

stem of my name capital, and juniper my lifeblood period

I take what's fair that I am hereby an elector

or does the audience prefer their lipstick applauded lavender?

what prose is their artillery drape over me, more drumtaps coroner

applause the aspen leaf strawberry scale me

what is a people but a sequel?

they invite me, yet buried in the moss I stay them secondhand

like I would join that pattern or stillwater walk away in plainest light

today my person is ago with humming stilts and wobble gait

who combs the timberline, there loves the birds who talon me

FIRST VERSE

Whereabouts a hearing
is my neighborhood

another pot another
empire sounds retire

furthering a blade
gainsays the yucca

that is grounds
of what abundance

republic will expire —

aflutter I asunder
it I freely

does the olive
slip asunder me

my symmetry geometry

authority me never

I am remainder
of my neighborly

I go upcountry
whose entry begins

wind whistle wind —

Free thought withal
the skys direction

mine uprose untitled
the entire prospect

of interrogations lost
on me American

enveloper by nature
whether nature be

big sky uncitizens
steep man amends

or is entire
I moves empty

light or birthright
mine whatever drone

in settlement I

blow my reed

CONSENSUS

This day of course
is reconciling you
American events
interior experience.

Hear the anthem means
the opportunity to speak.
In all cases there is feeling
that to remember the words

erase the history.
Twofolded pageantry:
a time inevitable
a fundamental world.

Employer of the chalkline, onlooker

concluder, please tell me keynote speaker,

which megaphone who greets me is my lover

blind to anyone I speak avoid finale

strikes my limbs nothing in pain corroding everafter

foreigner who isn't here to wonder

what steep man am I who suits your power,

I mind the appleseed I mute myself the redwood speaking

stands inside my uniform disrobe from me state motto

speaking prose that ends with listening, what's happening

is the approval, the decoy is that woman crush aluminum

which man first said my question, may I unfold consensus of my body

Free from my page the tabletop cicada

helicopter free the mower's blade

my time is what I venue

by my hand I carry by my ears an olive leaf

that comes the cloud and mountain, and goes to pipe

who whistles to a bird that I am being free

and people walk with love the gravel park

are they the subjects do they choose not to submit

who are at work and I old friendly hum

what laden bough that so much noise is foreigner

PASTORAL (ECLOGUE)

Tear down my cactus that I fell a child

wave my name thin stream no thicker than my hand

who splits the stone, I as the crow flies with the dragonfly

who hears that I am by their whirligig uncivilized

crow dawdles dragonfly and curtain pulses too

beside my windowpane from officers removed

that is great cinema, nor do I trim and stable

citizens or bees upripping roots unpublished

being without center, who goes elsewhere is the same

their elbow rests upon the balcony and drops a cigarette

that is my hand, that I roll up my sleeves over aluminum

is there a senator this far from their front door

who sings to justice keep thy eardrums at this hour

COMATAS

That I am listening to landscape

think of me midair, my atoms of the iron

made before my time in worker's hand

he lives with me, whomever he may be

are they defiant men who seek him

seeking to be sound, that is untested

clean from last night raining without cloud

what I surmise wet sockets styrofoams

that is a box mysterious to me

is wedged beneath a weed, with purpose

mine is to report these things

without superior, within the earshot

cloudy low horizons humming under heavy sky

is meant to be my only sentiment

opposing nothing that is witless

MY MANIFEST

Where do I stand that I will travel
is my love, do I turn people down

what hammer do I hear that knocks them down
who brought me in the basket, who speaks

no prose have I run after, no citizens
that is sound government that people leave

where I will have my country
somebody siren calls me back beneath my tree

my dog is buried here, that is I speak of liberty
what are my limbs that spring has taken them away

Candidate tobacco field voiceover
overgrows mudslide with chokecherry

all persons akimbo, I persons prone
so that I hear my name my absentee

in my condition, that I am one subject
subject to love and more or less one person

is the homeowner hiring the immigrant
what does she prize above her freedom

I love her anywhere careering with my eyes
from standstill to report both hands of her

she draws her bow and I is yet her citizen
she collects in cities disbelieves the public

rhetoric disrobes, its mistress with the torch
in notes of mint and aloe song refresh my store

POSTCARD

I place a czech koruna topmost rock in red rocks wilderness

my gum my glue

a bending bush

a little water carves around

what else is there

across the fog northwest Pacific where I sit

Cap Sante park in Anacortes

and I say my name Flamingo

softer than before,

I sponge the earth

returns to Tabor Park,

my basin of the world,

that is enough to bury my excrescence on the hill

my mind a stateless real to me than is the walking on

I pass the trail, continue with each thing as if before

how tall my shadow is the fact what fact to prove

and birds fall out the sky Las Vegas for example

just west of Taos, drive the mountain
name the thing wisteria which I have never seen
within a place I made but after nature
less I follow now if I believe
my ears a ringing time, that I wake up
with hollow eggs a nest or not what dug the trunk's saguaro
and my life as it were thick with water
air approach my fire turn my wrist to sage and more
Wisconsin forest touch of death
and Tropicana where I walk, just say I'm passing through
the pigeons die most every time
the bobcat hunts for food, I see its scat on narrow trail

GALLUP, NM, I-25

piedmont caked with rain the clod and pebble

reddest bluff in town real town Thoreau

his angel lips and journal world which exit is Theocritus

which is it now, the rubber oak or great Democracy

the ocotillo or peyote sound continue here

that is the resident Democracy, who bends the spoon

and blows a creek to dry —

I weigh myself as citizen or spirit

I am the substance of both

a river's floating light I float to bottom

newborn leaf pale red and weightless branch

my neighbor's hand the candle lighting

if I tumble down

one song from resurrection,

a man walks up his steps to mine

or eats the dung his honest song,

and nipping at my heels a country boy

in creosote include the world withstand it how

if I have only water

finishing with every leaf is laid upon the dusty ground

rescue nothing I have written of a song —

SAUNTERER

I see a halo pond, the algae sways

sit down with me its says —

the branch that is to say its name

untangles all authority —

I moth a star I crow a crosswalk

afternoon more real for cloudy day —

this day no record stands

wellspring the subject of the soul —

that I that once behind is fettered justly

throw concrete into an exhalation — ·

that I room for who one step ahead

is westing what abode so-called

my windows open to the dead.

ARGYLE, WI

dank wetness grey and pooling grass with rain

my soul too fat to watch,

I am an only child

driftless zone

I light the windows up,

my window let the air I'm living in

enough erupt the road —

I wade my feet

I drop my self

my next to none what empty

rumor of the world's demise,

the mower's bud,

bud I am incapable of listing

laden bough in lieu of me

of all the animals,

I live the desert,

excalibur or luxor light the core

on one side waxing moon

light on the other

angel's journal

"path was unexpectedly divine"

LONDON AFTERWARDS

the blade before its time
the blade on time
St. Michael rule the picture

shaft my light
Mojave Dust
my shadow dust a dime

the Hoover dam last boughs
and limbs last gleaming mine
Mt. Hood fly south forever

time must be
the lowest note
must I become divine

THE TRAVEL POEM

I walk the room to pioneer

I cross the bridge for what

should I who walk with god

if walker plucks no wild fruit

it ends right now nonfiction —

water through its source back into dust

disturb the dunes soft cake

a stepping through

the park is built in Paradise —

completes the speaking —

walled-in pond in its entire depth —

what else if not the resurrection

sunray spiny daisy mind

I nap beneath the apricots

sunray spiny daisy mind

my barren mind Democracy —

my deadly hand all things I touch rename

my o and o writ into aspen

same I share with atom and the nature back away

and goes the world away that knew the names I gave

in one of my translations that can happen

write me over now —

from o to atom —

Andover room —

being without center

who goes elsewhere is the same

dry empty pool the bluest light

new life to live that gives Americans the name

in prose resist that first abode

in license of real death,

which happens trust the walking no one walking here

in reservoirs of water paved across the sky

that everyone is lived and lights their grave

around Democracy,

outside of paradise,

that ends the evening land and goes to pipe

who stares the branch away —

and like the person I could not forgive,

that is forgotten —

Mojave Desert Star

the aster valley sage

cliff cactus shafting light

Sonora Dust

in spirit not the hand,

as any boy would say is not the case —

first be American, first interrupt oneself —

I am one song from resurrection

cholla boughs the diamonds rot

their skin becoming rain come here

I am behind the day modernity

with yucca thousand times in bloom

a bottle found I caught the moth,

I broke coyote's paw,

and in a world where this can happen

every hand becomes two-handed engine

bury me within synonymous the mind is blank —

HAWTHORNE BLVD.

Face of the road before
the afternoon, where women
like two birds are gone
with hesitation
as I carry them a soft
memory of their passing:

Remember the trees,
as though the aftermath
replayed our introduction,
the theory overlapping
theory, like a bird?

The women in one word:
the mystery of their shared bodies
near the ratio of their names.
I know them no more than I
may answer my own question:

Is it day or transcript
of another day or not
the ambush, afternoon?

BATTUS (TO AMARYLLIS)

Once it begins, the score is obvious.

White vines with wildflowers spring

along the fence, our center. Syntax folds,

the ballot shrinks into a coin and flips

the dews suspend us and we kiss ourselves

and cannot touch our noses. I love listening.

What awful noise, that is the bride's a bride

where we are minor, swift. I bless our fence.

Ornamental light. Who's there, a pox

to love's decay, a day away from day?

As proud participants – a sampled weight

of bleeding ray? *Her curfew crushed the world.*

Then it was richer, a corridor to heaven

equivalent and loved, an encore. *Dove.*

Where we have history, there is insistent

garnishing with parsley, evenings

of famine, a starlet's bra removed

by scientists in drag. And there you are,

Amaryllis, whose duck-duck-goose unrolls

calling us to wonder. *Love's sacred bunker*.

There are many greens. The machine
is self-sufficient. And here I pipe a drop
in pressure. Ancillary, I drive below
the ether, slipping stony thoughts.
"What's alive is lovely," "Like patterns over
time." Shorelines the aspen flutter, revive,
cool beneath some clouds, I sample
Walden Pond this global noon. I say Amaryllis
with binary effectiveness: open

sesame,   *repeat*,   open season
for the sake of Battus.   *Repeat*:
Battus. Amaryllis, let speak my eyes.

THE NEW POEM

I am the brag this early hour

west whichever way is west lets go

•

I report what one may see if they too stare away

I follow through their skin

there is my kingdom valley butte where I hold sway

the starbuck and the ratany I go there all the time

•

release the blow I walk a windy path

the same that once my one vocation

where a path a limestone quarry offs the path

I tore the books now I press on

each I less than I am a man in tatters paid

•

white apache plume my publicist sun-throated

my reception waits, my model will descend to him some day

inside my soul like-minded king take root

a deviant in costume green a shining child

snake he slips my earring off and rides the horse of flame

or eats the dung his honest song

•

my cup I won from Battus kill who sleeps the era down

him running me his publications,

him days away disaster,

I accept his olive smoke and nothing after it

I walk away the lemon groves that smoke in COLIN's name

I will survive one more than I

you ask me my vocation

see police are landing choppers on your gardened little head

THE MARGINIST

marginist my soul

        free standing arch —

a walled-in pond

        two inches deep —

a yucca stalk

        a shepherd's hook —

a prose inept

        begin —

THYRSIS

A baby blew a kiss to my lips.

Doorbell on the inside of a hive.

Blink with me, like Jonah and the Whale

with each other. Bride to be: be loved.

Bring me the milk, the sun is fielding limes.

You wore me out of handing you the curb.

Ace of elms in our cards,   we doubt

nonetheless. A country falls apart.

Tomato berry, grow inside this horse.

Sing as if the note were cherry, crudely.

A barrel holds the night and day apart.

Our minds admit the sun. My times times one.

HOBBINOLL

Sweet soul. On loan with every hour,

every story, hope blink ahead

and lead me where to go.

For Corydon my keeper rest his soul

I sing what he would hear: *Words*

raise this cup against my lips, a blip.

Aphasia will return

with someone else: Hobbinoll's my name,

it hovers, it enhances what it dances

dead: *a name, a lullaby,* sweet Comatas:

"Hold on to what you spur, its future is

your chance, a precious droplet entering

a gallery from pleasant rain." I'm game.

Into the sunlight we all speak Amaryllis

on cue, like windchimes in a siege. . .

LYCIDAS

Asymmetrical star, vibrantly
renewed. In comparison to waking
up a cloud, or rather walking up
the street. There is no universe but ours

and theirs. Our common song is optional.
Holy puddle, distilling Adam's time
with Eve's collage. We will fail, like
a summer toque, one that falls below

the nose. Plastic hammer. Paradise
of picked teams, in eeny meeny
rows. Away we go: let's build it all
again. The vote will be announced in psalms.

And do I steer the wrath away,

ocotillo thorn thrust out the eye of god

ground crack open god no more

two million for a million of my hair

I am one song from resurrection

wish it true, ask god the question

and the form of god returns no subject

flare of copper stone his lazy hand unbend

Bygone a room damp street the rain remade

for I am yet a child, and one song I sing

Jerusalem my lamp the catclaw powder

tamarisk a crowded house is god the same I hear

JERUSALEM

Take my hand into another number
is the reason animates the olive pit
grace me adoringly whatever is my partner
all the same I am to breathe unfiltered air

what is complete is in composite
is a person first to last my bark strips bare
among the people that are rid of me
disturb the pond a million needles more

I am typing with the wind upon a cactus
speaks my eyes in streaks of what America before
what is eponymous is there the traffic lights
my walking lights of yellow grasses bending

THE YOUNG HERDSMAN

Bird I love but one who floats to thee,

prefers to be the jade where there is none

with quiet time, how often am I thereby green

I pay the officer one look I go inside

I speak to her I love, that is my habit —

love opens the acorn of my earshot state

these notes I carry in my arms now please

for love who is already short of breath

more people hear, love whisper through the air

what have I to do with their interrogations

chain me down that I no wonder would undo

my love is light a silent window

and the riverbed, that is my skin

Love is the country, tell me the foreigner

who speaks what is this made for me my love

what love captains of cedar, what man is an alliance

I have my person wrap me

love is sage and tar and rips apart my hand

I am an empty glass love rings am I in uniform

I roll my sleeves of course love melts me head to toe

to hold myself straight, and that crumbles the authority

what liberty please would the keynote speaker

swooping for I hear, who sings to me this land is yours

what love have I will be my currency

and lives uncredited, anonymous

Oncoming love do I slip into uniform

or censor speaking love in custody

my loving name outpours to people her

within her harbor, and she twice elected from the pond

love's letters overlay the blue

forever which is unbelievable repay her

TWO IDYLLS

The Aftermap

of us entire,

both my neighbor and unknown to me

my walking one strict boundary

    the visible beyond,

    this nation

        first to be ongoing

        independence underneath no single power

The Irredenta

each person-making image of these states

is empire   empire is sound

without audience

           one sound circumference

is the bee that brings me honey where I

verdict and example of America

SAME SUBJECT CONTINUED

Organizing not a word to be explained in time,

footsteps in the snow unfreezing,

member of no address

speaking on no behalf, I roll my eyes so slightly

bite the oak, mind

my person bare,

citizen the man

the same with pebbles,

now granted power I assemble

half my hearing sound —

I pull a person with an oar this person is so stately

I describe myself and I,

with this my trace, I write this paper plain —

I comes to hand

laden bough in lieu

of nation of what

sounds good sailing

worth itself that is a respiration

       Stateless…

                                 Fullness…

I administers this world

the helicopter's way

flowers the flag

redeems the reprobate

who names discover

this America

this witless purpose

. . .and again the song. . .

I for example

I moves empty

must I correspond

my blasted century. withdraw

the first to interrupt oneself

Henry do I unclose the acorn

rights are method or the field.

All is note.

KEELAN (WALK)

stranger,

                 leaf

      astray

of all desire for the liquidated soul,

                      fellow author

in the customary,

     resist this way across the page

          green-lending I is in between

POUND (WALK)

to be a priest,

        same

      to spell the words accordingly

until there is no unit of reflection,

          no Little I who is ecstatic o

    no Little I who after all is all

      of this assembly,

        and yet no more

         the wrath

THAT ALL EXPENSE. . .

that grows aloud one afternoon unearth a floating —

louder I describe my revelations

              less I hold within my eyes —

      that I asunder see my hands and nothing terminal a country

is remembered for its depth of prose and stable freedoms

      from invalid description
      comes nothing uncertain

      save the stroke of sunlight
      happens to recall exhaustion

Whitman words —

    do shepherds now insist upon perfection learn my strummers hand

AFTER TANTIVY

I am exotic blank

as amorous as pendulous to them

who will be officers

of ordinary life

the lover of the ocean in my ears

an ocean in my ears

Which of them pull over paddling with me

inside a loving that's a hearing evermore?

The object is America's great furnaces

The subject tells the object it will be my will

Motherless goddamn modernity never grew

INSCRIPTION (OR EPITAPH)

I am the silhouette the same as no one

the example of the cloud,

I am the same who will be after death

a pond blown over be blown back to rest

a pond to kiss my feet, so sure is west

however strict the terms may be forever slipping

east behold a sparrow lives with me —

a blunt true mover out of hand —

unlanguage here a post I stand —

The same subject continued

poem laughing stand beyond the god

is English grazing the uncredited

a politics a wither poetry

I pick people off the ground I citizened

the boy grew taller than his statue

who uniforms the child with the man

they are then idle from my listening :

rescue nothing I have written of a song —

ACKNOWLEDGEMENTS

Thank you to the journals in which the following poems appeared:

The New England Review
  "The Young Herdsman"

VOLT
  "First Verse" (published as "Theocritean")
  "Keelan (Walk)"
  "Pound (Walk)"
  "Inscription (or Epitaph)"

Fence
  "After Tantivy"
  "The Same Subject Continued"

The Colorado Review
  "Jerusalem"

The Antioch Review
  "Shepherd's Song"

Lana Turner Journal
  "Hobbinoll" (published as "Sweet soul. On loan in every hour")
  "New Poem"
  "Two Idylls"

Blackbox Manifold
  "Thyrsis" (published as "A baby blew a kiss to my lips.")

Weekday
  "Once it begins, the score is obvious" (included in "Battus (to Amaryllis)")

Gobbet
    "There are many greens. The machine" (included in "Battus
    (to Amaryllis)")

New American Writing
    "Hawthorne Blvd."

The Laurel Review
    "Lycidas" (published as "Asymmetrical star, vibrantly")

Also thank you to Kathryn Kruse and Theresa White from Residency on the Farm for years of support. The poem "Argyle, WI" is dedicated to you.

Thank you to Andrews Nicholson and Merecicky, as well as Colby Gillette for all your shared considerations of poetry across our friendships. Joe, Kelly, and Kate, thank you for the drinks and the keno. Don and Claudia: you've done me far too much.

Finally, thanks to Stephen, Kazim, and Lindsey for supporting this work, as well as everyone else at Nightboat.

OSCAR OSWALD's poetry has appeared in *The Antioch Review*, *Colorado Review*, *Denver Quarterly*, *Blackbox Manifold*, and *Fence*, among other journals. He has a PhD in English and Creative Writing from the University of Nevada, Las Vegas, where he was a Black Mountain Fellow. He has also served as an assistant editor for Noemi Press and as the poetry editor for Witness.

NIGHTBOAT BOOKS

Nightboat Books, a nonprofit organization, seeks to develop audiences for writers whose work resists convention and transcends boundaries. We publish books rich with poignancy, intelligence, and risk. Please visit nightboat.org to learn about our titles and how you can support our future publications.

The following individuals have supported the publication of this book. We thank them for their generosity and commitment to the mission of Nightboat Books:

Kazim Ali
Anonymous (4)
Abraham Avnisan
Jean C. Ballantyne
The Robert C. Brooks Revocable Trust
Amanda Greenberger
Rachel Lithgow
Anne Marie Macari
Elizabeth Madans
Elizabeth Motika
Thomas Shardlow
Benjamin Taylor
Jerrie Whitfield & Richard Motika

This book is made possible, in part, by grants from the New York City Department of Cultural Affairs in partnership with the City Council and the New York State Council on the Arts Literature Program.